I CAN READ ABOUT
DINOSAURS

Written by John Howard

Illustrated by Judith Fringuello

Troll Associates

Millions of years ago, when much of the world was warm and swampy, strange-looking reptiles called dinosaurs roamed the earth.

The first dinosaurs were not very big.

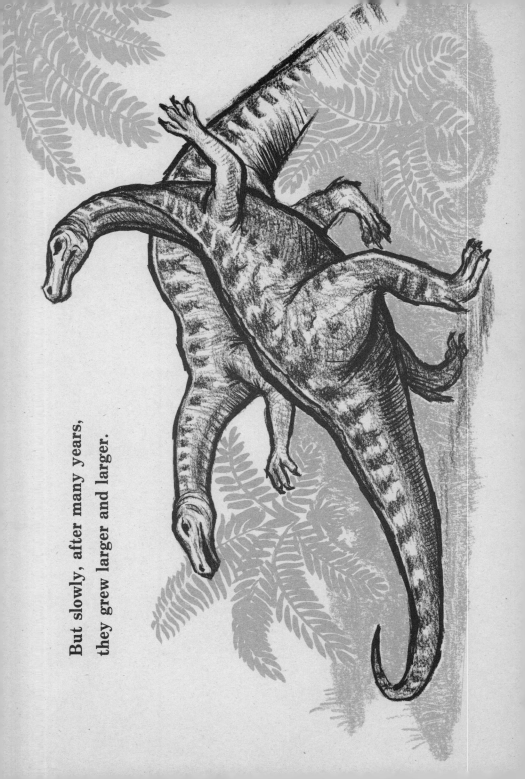

But slowly, after many years, they grew larger and larger.

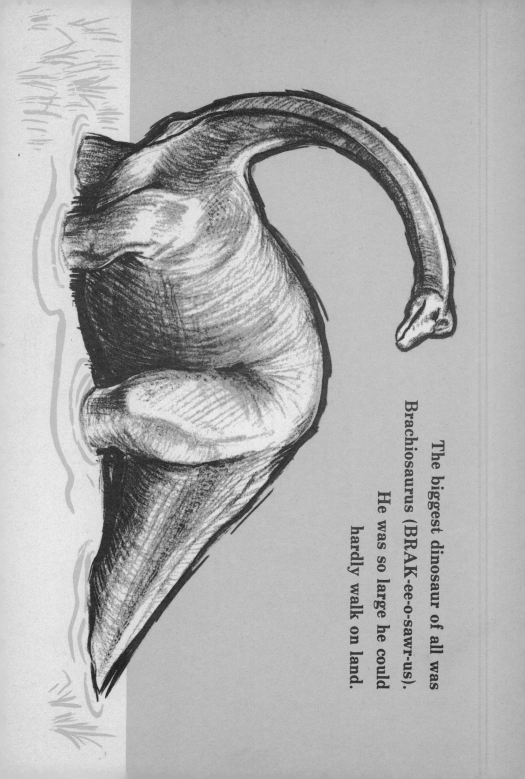

The biggest dinosaur of all was
Brachiosaurus (BRAK-ee-o-sawr-us).
He was so large he could
hardly walk on land.

A dinosaur almost as large was Brontosaurus (BRON-toe-sawr-us). He had a very long neck and tail.

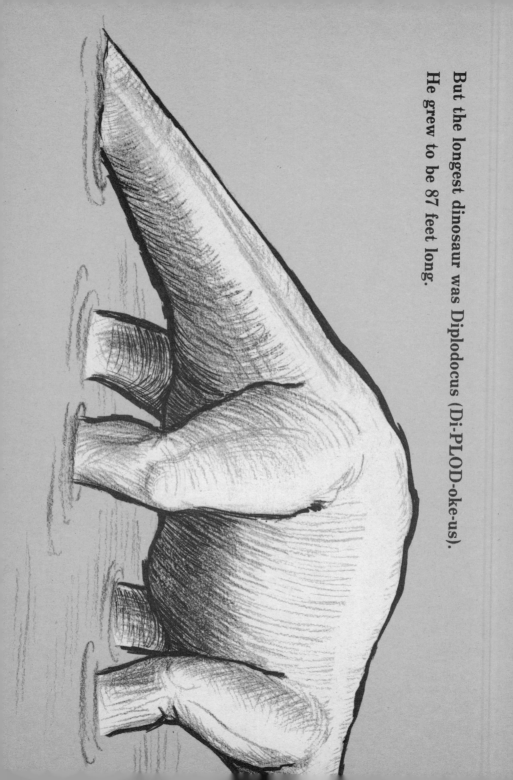

But the longest dinosaur was Diplodocus (Di-PLOD-oke-us).
He grew to be 87 feet long.

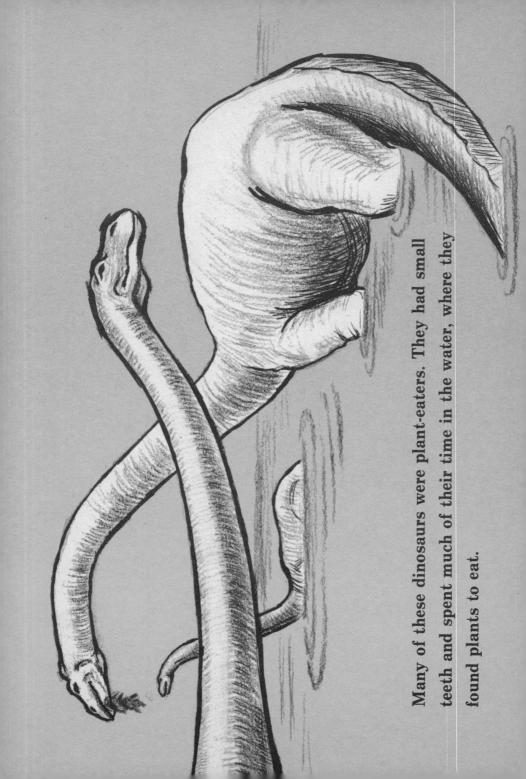

Many of these dinosaurs were plant-eaters. They had small teeth and spent much of their time in the water, where they found plants to eat.

But meat-eating dinosaurs did not like water. They had big strong teeth and stayed on land, hunting food.

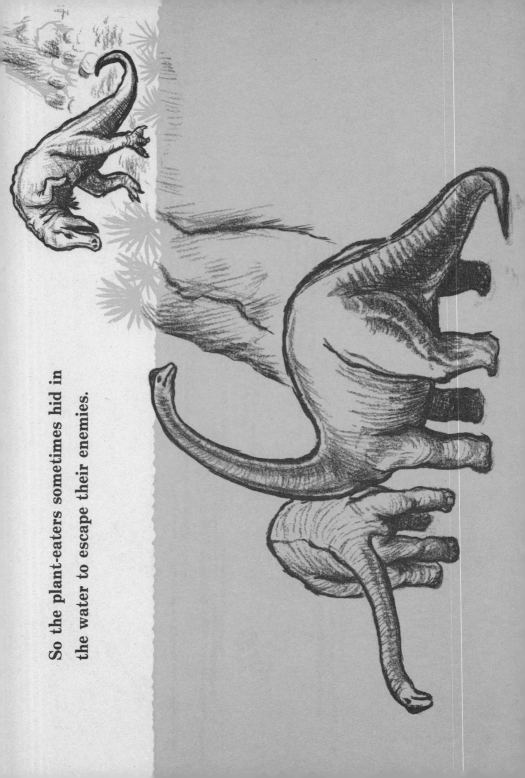

So the plant-eaters sometimes hid in the water to escape their enemies.

One of the most dangerous meat-eaters was Allosaurus (AL-o-sawr-us).

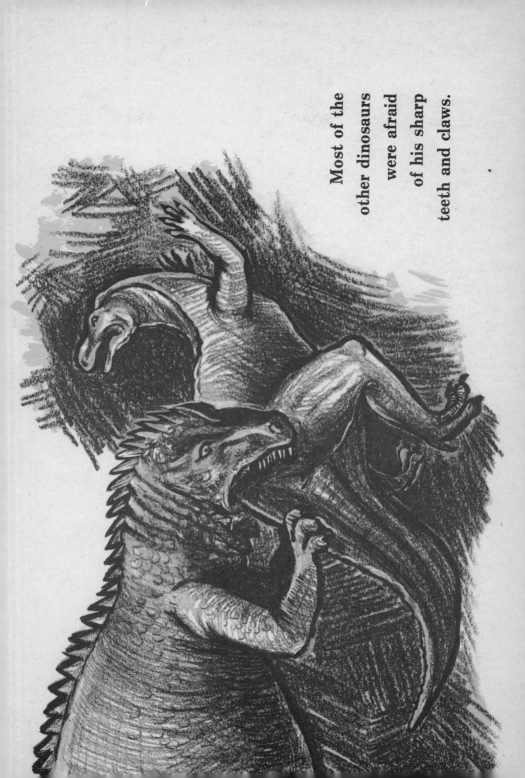

Most of the
other dinosaurs
were afraid
of his sharp
teeth and claws.

STEGOSAURUS

ALLOSAURUS

But some plant-eaters had armor for protection.

When Stegosaurus (STEG-o-sawr-us) swung his spiked tail, Allosaurus learned to leave him alone.

After many years, Allosaurus died out. But a bigger and more terrible giant, called Tyrannosaurus Rex (Tie-RAN-o-sawr-us rex), took his place. His teeth were over 5 inches long!

Trachodon (TRAK-o-don) had a lot of teeth too, but they were very small, and he used them to grind up plants. His duck-billed mouth was very useful for digging up food in the mud under water.

The meat-eaters could usually run much faster than the plant-eaters. If Tyrannosaurus Rex caught Trachodon before he could escape to the water,

there would be
a terrible battle!

But sometimes there
were plant-eaters who
could fight mighty
Tyrannosaurus. One of
these was Triceratops
(Tri-SER-a-tops).

With his long, pointed horns and the bony shield behind his head, he could defend himself very well.

Ankylosaurus (An-KILL-o-sawr-us) was covered with thick, bony plates. Even Tyrannosaurus could not bite through that!

But as large as they were, these dinosaurs had very tiny brains. Their brains were about the size of a kitten's.

In the sea and in the sky, other strange reptiles were living at the time of the dinosaurs.

Those in the sky had leathery or scaly skin instead of feathers. They were meat-eaters who could swoop down to catch smaller reptiles and fish.

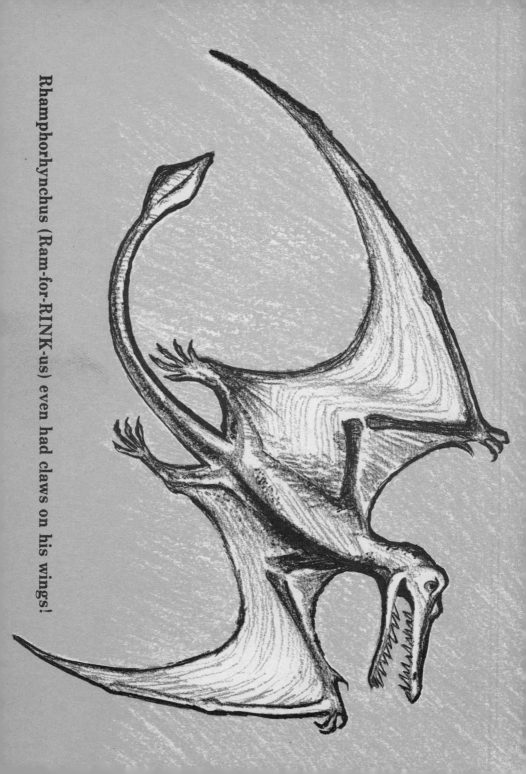

Rhamphorhynchus (Ram-for-RINK-us) even had claws on his wings!

Many of the reptiles living
in the sea looked like sea serpents.
Elasmosaurus (Ee-LAZ-mo-sawr-us)
sometimes grew to be 40 or 50 feet long.

After living for over 100 million years, these great animals began to die out. Finally, they vanished from the face of the earth.

No one is sure why they died. Some scientists think the weather turned colder, and there were not enough plants to eat.

Others believe that smaller animals ate the dinosaur eggs. The dinosaurs probably could not adapt themselves to these and other changes.

But as the dinosaurs disappeared, other animals called mammals took their place.

The mammals were small at first, but after the dinosaurs had vanished, they began to grow and change.

1. EOHIPPUS — size of a fox

2. MESOHIPPUS — size of a sheep

3. MERYCHIPPUS size of a Shetland pony

4. PLIOHIPPUS — size of a donkey

5. EQUUS — size of a domestic horse

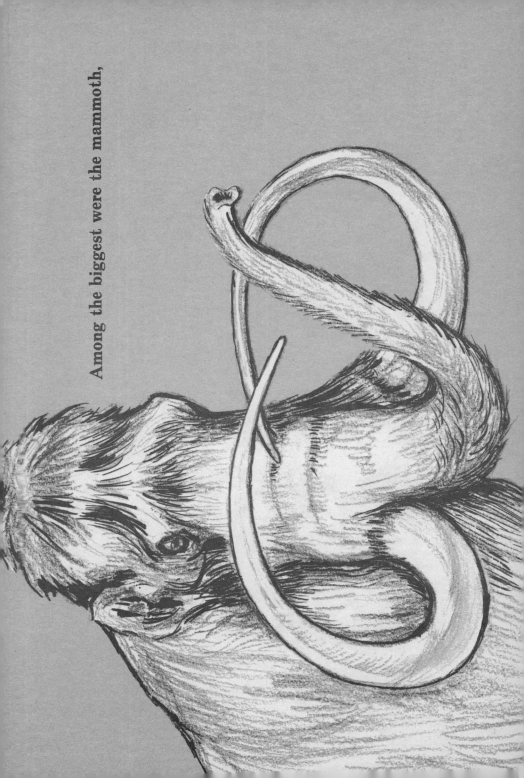

Among the biggest were the mammoth,

and his close cousin, the mastodon.

One of the fiercest
mammals was the sabre-toothed tiger.
Even the mammoths were afraid of his big teeth.

Soon after man appeared on earth, most of these early mammals died out too. It may have been because the weather turned colder again, and there was not enough food.

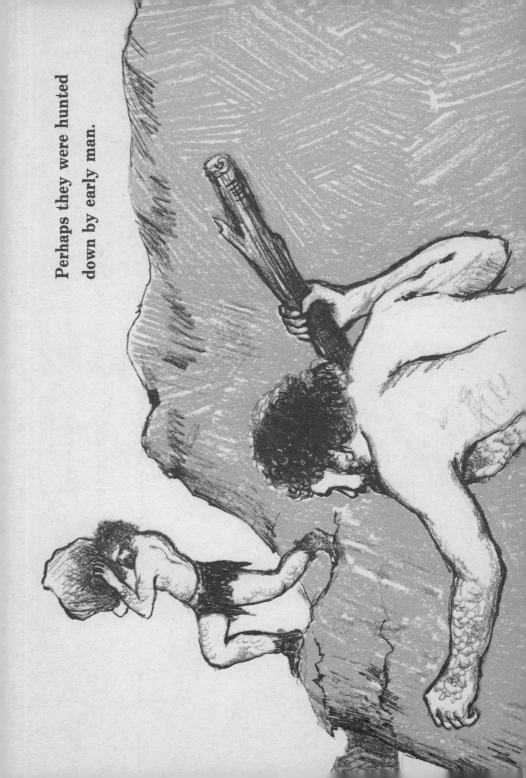

Perhaps they were hunted down by early man.

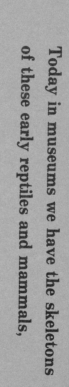

Today in museums we have the skeletons
of these early reptiles and mammals,

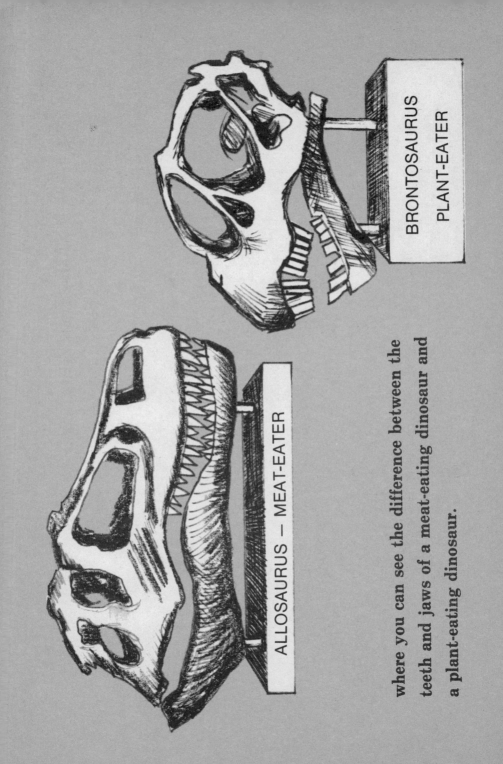

BRONTOSAURUS
PLANT-EATER

ALLOSAURUS — MEAT-EATER

where you can see the difference between the teeth and jaws of a meat-eating dinosaur and a plant-eating dinosaur.

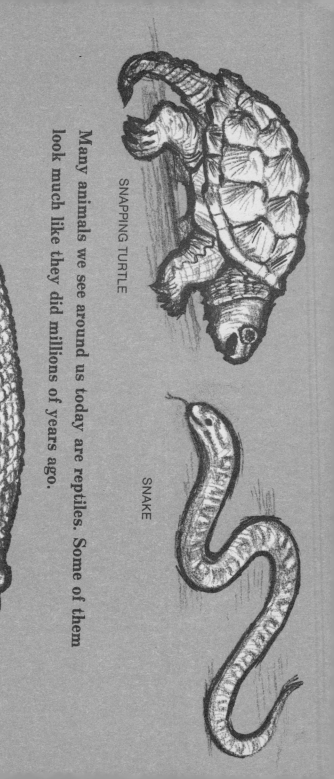

SNAPPING TURTLE

SNAKE

ALLIGATOR

Many animals we see around us today are reptiles. Some of them look much like they did millions of years ago.

In fact, a lizard looks a lot like a tiny dinosaur.

Scientists have learned about dinosaurs and other animals from bones and impressions discovered in rocks. These are called fossils. New fossils are still being discovered all over the world.

Fossils may teach us more about the dinosaurs and why they disappeared. They may even tell us about other prehistoric animals that have not been discovered yet.